A THOUSAND PROFANE PIECES

A THOUSAND
PROFANE PIECES

Myna Wallin

Tightrope Books, 2006

Toronto ⊕ Detroit

Tightrope Books
17 Greyton Crescent
Toronto, Ontario
Canada M6E 2G1
www.tightropebooks.com

Editor: Ray Hsu
Typesetting: Carleton Wilson
Cover art: D. Bigham
Author photo: D. Bigham

Printed and bound in Canada

LIBRARY AND ARCHIVES CANADA
CATALOGUING IN PUBLICATION

Wallin, Myna
A thousand profane pieces / Myna Wallin; editor , Ray Hsu.

Poems.
ISBN 0-9738645-3-2

1. Erotic poetry, Canadian (English). I. Hsu, Ray, 1978–
II. Title.

PS8595.A5699T56 2006   C811'.6   C2006-902197-X

In memory of my parents, Sam & Esther

CONTENTS

⊞ IN THE THROES

Trophy Poets   11
One-Word Answers   13
Mid-Life Crisis in Ft. Lauderdale   14
Three for the Road   16
Screen Vixen   18
An Incident   19
The Self-Improvement Revolution   20
Sleight of Hand   21
"Love?"   22

⊞ Casting Call

The Other Young Ones   25
An Object Lesson   26
Resurrections   27
Softer than Angora   28
The Decline of Modern Conversation   29
Unrequited & Co.   31
This Is my Beer Commercial   32
Classified: 34
Theorizing the Postmodern   35
Smooth as Pearls   37
Take Me   38
Even Divas Get the Blues   39
Of Course the Popcorn Helps, Too   42

▣ Off-Limits

Animal Passion   45
A Few Terminal D's   46
Wildlife   47
Klezmer Music on Christmas Eve   48
This Won't Hurt a Bit   49
The Old Abandonment   50
Mid-Life Crisis in Ft. Lauderdale, Revisited   51
Secret Lives   54
The Meek Shall Inherit   56
House of Cards   57
The Pear   58
Meditation on a Photograph   59
None of This   60
Warning Signs   61

▣ An Aerial View

Three Bodies   65
An Email About the Ocean   67
Providence, Rhode Island   68
Sonnet for John   69
The Angel Effect   70
Transcendence   71

Section 1

IN THE THROES

TROPHY POETS

They're all the rage—
    blondes are out; thinkers are in
proclaims a Toronto Life cover story:
    spotted at important cocktail parties
a copy of Carson's *Men in the Off Hours*
    poking out of knapsacks, talking Griffin & Trillium,
vigorously debating the merits of sound
    poetry.

Doctors, lawyers, take their trophy poets
    to the South of France or cottages on Lake Rosseau.
Fake boobs are out; they want a woman with big
    opinions, with Bohemian flair. Holt Renfrew ladies

are threatened, commenting poisonously on the "Sally Anne girls,"
    during a glycolic peel or paraffin treatment. These men
in suits, appetites wander. This is the new urban pairing.
    The men need some culture, some social relevance, a connection
to the arts beyond symphony tickets. For their part, the poets
    admire men who can escort them to Scaramouche or Canoe

withdrawing 50s and 100s, manicured hands dipping into Gucci
    leather. Yet, the new women feel strangely
objectified. A professional was overheard whispering, "My little
    poet laureate," to his girlfriend, just published in *Grain*.
Some of these bankers have poetic aspirations: when they bring
a sonnet or haiku to the table the romance is dead.

Trophy poets are coming, there's no stopping them. Cartier
        watches they didn't buy with royalties peek out
from under their black Gap turtlenecks. Seen
        getting out of SUV's looking self-conscious, morally
conflicted. They are so clever,
        these girls, if you stare into their pupils long enough

        it's foreplay.

ONE-WORD ANSWERS

Kevin. Percussionist. Paris.
And one-word questions:
You? Drink? Later?
When responses come he's

smoke rings trailing pianissimo,
eyeing his options as women
hover. He drinks too fast,
his eyes are agate blue.

She's a ripe pomegranate,
straining against the pith.
Her irises open to let him in.

MID-LIFE CRISIS IN FT. LAUDERDALE

It's time to pierce my nose
go to a rave, try ecstasy
to keep the essence of youth
from slipping away

I thought time was a cosmetic
illusion, kept subtracting years
so long as the coverup covered
up, so long as the man opposite me
was too young to take life seriously

It's time for Botox but I can't make the leap
from dabbing on makeup to freezing
muscles, lines of experience
like lines of a poem I refuse
to erase

Every year I am further from Spring
Break madness, inevitable as the tide:
girls in bikinis which get tinier,
boys' suits get bigger but lower slung,
they toss footballs & drink American beer
grateful for advances in silicone
and that teenage girls don't heed
skin cancer warnings
baking in the sun like paprika-burnt
free-range chickens

Someone up in the sky got a pilot license
to fly a helicopter all day
IGUANA'S WET BIKINI CONTEST GIRLS DRINK FREE

I'm supposed to be married by now or divorced
or both, girls of that age my daughters
earning self-reflected credit for their beauty
& doling out advice in preserving it

Instead I'm reading *The Girl's Guide to Hunting &*
Fishing, trying to conjure my youth with
as much success as Houdini had
in contacting his mother

I reel in a paunchy, coffee-bean coloured
My name is Reynaldo
extending a thick hand heavy with gold rings
You look so beautiful
eyes languidly taking in the areas my bathing
suit doesn't conceal

I have forgotten Spanish
& he has learned only pick-up English—
I throw this one back,
lift my beach towel raining hot sand,
grab a slopey big hat &
wander until I see a crowd forming,
following a Manatee who has drifted
too close to shore by mistake.

THREE FOR THE ROAD

The Fast Ride:

There are those who like to whip
and those who like to be whipped—
like Pozzo & Lucky
like Bonnie & Clyde
some of us are along for the ride

The slow cruise, the fast lane
whether you're coming
or going
it's the same old game

The Fast Life:

Fast men in their fast cars
with women who fast
into size twos,
brains malnutritioned—
it's not that they're stupid
there just isn't enough vitamin B
to replace decaying brain cells

Fast Forward:

She stood out in the crowd
like a hooker at the Taj Mahal
like a socialite at Hollywood & Vine

She was devoured constantly
by desperate paparazzi eyes
that followed her
like a trick painting

Everywhere that Mary goes
the sheep are sure to want her

SCREEN VIXEN

I'd like to mold my body
into the one up on the screen:
breasts pushed up and out,
posing together—

big pouty red lips,
someone on hand to do constant touchups,
soft flowing hair,
a face that stays cool & powdered
even while I hobble, stiletto-heeled, down the
cobblestone road,
toward a man, lying face-down in his own blood.

I'd like to have the breasts, legs, pout
that stops a man dead in his tracks.

AN INCIDENT

You walk out your front door.
You see a bunch of firemen, smell smoke.
There are a dozen fire trucks and an air
of hysteria on the usually quiet street.

Your first thought: will the cat be alright?
You ask a fireman, *Should I leave my cat?*
He says *We're pretty good*
and you wonder if that's really an answer.

You see huge hoses aimed at the German
Embassy two doors down,
get an irresistible urge to talk to the
journalists, but you've got nothing to say.

You sense this is a very big deal
when you see 17 still photographers
capturing the blaze with 2-foot long zooms.
Even though you're choking on smoke

watching the drama unfold, you suddenly realize
you slept through sirens from 12 fire trucks,
6 police cars and 2 ambulances, wonder how
that is possible. You can taste the adrenalin

as police scour the Embassy and the surrounding area
for the arsonist. You watch the six o'clock news,
relieved to find out it wasn't you.

THE SELF-IMPROVEMENT REVOLUTION

I'm learning to lucid dream,
be powerful in and out of my conscious awareness,
in and out of my boa-feathered baby dolls.

There are more ways to improve
than I can count carbs or free weight reps:
learn Pilates, French, arrange flowers, meditate.
Find my Chi. My G-spot. Take Kabbalah classes.

I used to see psychics,
tried rolfing and sensory deprivation tanks in the 80s.
No more past-life regression for me,
nothing that digs so deep.

It's all about the self-empowerment, baby,
and he'll never know what hit him.
I'm so centered I can walk in my Jimmy Choos
and snort a little coke at parties like Kate Moss,
while repeating daily
"I am perfect, whole and beautiful."

Women, if they stay single long enough,
become bounty hunters—
they'll stake you out, take you home, tie you up—
long before any dinner conversation.

Self-improvement as salvation
is the modern woman's revolution.
It has its myths, like any other,
such as strength and self-sufficiency. Also
"the more you evolve, the more you'll be loved."

SLEIGH OF HAND

Prozac is for eunuchs. A plot, he says,
denying paranoia. *The doctors
get rich from my misery.* His voice

petulant, nothing wrong
with him except his stock
options, his bonds.

Distract him with silk scarves,
with flowers, with how I saw
myself in half to hold him spellbound.

He regresses, his 6-year-old self,
an aching arrhythmia, a loneliness
jutting deep, a scar tissue.

I want to tear his darkness away,
a magician who seizes the black cloth
from an empty cage, revealing doves.

"LOVE?"

I dreamed of a spelling bee, I was applauding
and you were up next.

MONOGAMY the judge intoned.
Repeat, you said.

You scraped by with M-O-, sounding it out, N-O-,
finding Latin roots, G-A-, gasping, A-M-Y?

Your opponent spelled DISPOSABLE
so quickly I thought he was showing off.

ETERNITY. Perspiring, you looked stymied,
bewildered even,

and I felt sorry for you.
You weren't expecting such hard words.

Section 2

CASTING CALL

THE OTHER YOUNG ONES

You look like Cat Stevens.
—*Who?*

Fresh, unspoiled, tangle of black curls,
        eyes of a zealot,

in the '70s young men wore
        tight faded denim falling apart by degrees,

anti-establishment, no logos. A guitar
in one hand, hash pipe in the other.

I remember the boys in my Renaissance class looking
like a touring production of *Hair*—

free, naked and beautiful. That's what you remind me of—
        a childhood I never had, your bicycle shorts,

skateboard career, maybe your *Tour de France* gold,
        and me, my gray roots showing, drunk on gin & tonics.

"Live fast, live hard." A method actor I once loved
        followed Jim Dean's credo. "Live fast, die young."

You remind me of him, somehow, and the other young ones,
        the Cheshire cats, their hard teeth grinning in the dark.

AN OBJECT LESSON

Power-dressing at 23: fishnets, garter-belts,
fuck-me pumps, the makeup of evangelists.
A cab driver ogles, *You should be Miss America,*
and the horror flick director: *lose the shirt.*
Before she knows it makes her flush,
she's undoing buttons, unhooking her bra.
The director again, *Polaroid her,* caffeinated,
to the kid who's died and gone to PA heaven
where pretty women remove their shirts on command,
to star in some low-budget piece-of-shit
financed by periodontists looking for tax shelters.
Everybody's happy except the boyfriend,
You call that acting? And her, crying
even though her agent said it would lead
to bigger things. She gives it up to enroll
in school—her professor of Moral Philosophy
propositions her and she's back to the mirror
to guess what she's worth, counting
pores, assessing change. And later,
men will treat her with respect, not lust,
and she'll wonder *which was worse?*

RESURRECTIONS

My mother is alive again
in my dreams.
And so is my father,
though they rarely appear together.

In one variation
my mother returns to visit,
her cancer healed.
We talk for a bit & she whispers
Don't tell your father I was here.

I ask her why she doesn't stay,
admit, embarrassed,
I thought you were dead.
No, there's no such thing & laughs lightly
though she can't explain why her visits
are so infrequent.

Immortality makes sense at night.
My father's heart seems strong again
as he rushes around with purpose.
Sometimes he tells me not to worry.
It will be alright.

My mother though is still frail,
and we hold each other, rocking.
In the morning I'm startled that
I remember her touch—
the exact pressure of her hand on mine.

SOFTER THAN ANGORA

At twelve my mother taught me to discriminate
between silk crepe & crushed velvet, silver plate
& sterling. She ordered flocked wallpaper for my
bedroom, taught me cashmere by touch—much softer
than angora.

A collector of antiques, oil paintings, dozens of enameled
teacups etched in gold, fluted champagne glasses,
the Art Nouveau salt shaker. Perfection lived in a pair
of silver sugar tongs. Her collection, her three children:

Sheilah chose a screen to conceal her amnesia,
Dick got the dishes, gold and in storage, and I
chose an embroidered tapestry to hang in place of her,
lovers in Sunday wear, on English grass, hangs
in my bedchamber now, their dog and their picnic
basket, their cherubs in the trees.

THE DECLINE OF MODERN CONVERSATION

We drink bottle after bottle of Italian white,
Pino Grigio, I think.
Dry and sophisticated, satirical,
like this little party.

(We stay away from red as our host explains
it will wear a hole in your colon, eventually.)

After the 6th or 7th bottle,
We expose our neuroses, each by each.

This one is afraid of staplers and fax machines.
That one is turned on by Mormons.
She fantasizes about men from Down Under
(their Aussie-accented crocodile wrestling).

And we are all six degrees of separation from
Christian Bök.

It's a free-for-all, this decline of
modern conversation: depressives and
addicts of every kind.

Self-revelation is the game,
so I throw a bone—
something about acrylic paint
& a thing for trumpet players.

There are frequent trips to the washroom,
the patio outdoors for a toke, until

I could swear I saw collars on the men
with name tags & drool
pooling on the tabletop.

I want to be one of these women-in-control,
But I was born too early—
never mastered "walk the dog" on my yo-yo.

I feel dirty when I get home,
like I did after watching Isabelle Huppert
in *The Piano Teacher* (who begs her student to gag
her with her own stockings, beat her unconscious).

UNREQUITED & CO.

Ruth is still in love with Francesco, her ex.
She had to break it off because
he couldn't get Denise out of his head,

who in turn loved Sven, her ex,
while Sven unexpectedly loved Nathaniel, who was his ex—
And all the exes trailed off

like an Escher drawing,
                down and up
     a winding staircase that ended
& began on a four-tiered wedding cake.

As soon as a breakup is complete
each new ex shifts in position
becoming the one most pined for.

Proving hindsight is love's craftiest illusion
and, you've got to appreciate a little irony
now & then.

THIS IS MY BEER COMMERCIAL

In my perfect self-enclosed universe,
my sixty Andy Warhol seconds,
there are lots of gorgeous men
in tiny little European bathing suits.

Beautiful men, masculine & hip,
stand around a huge, uterine aquamarine pool.

(Okay, so my perfect universe is a little Freudian,
but aside from that it's heaven.)

The men are bringing the women cold beers,
in between diving and flexing,
and rippling through the water.

The women are wearing fabulous little Chanel suits,
Fortune 500 gals having a beer and a little
divertissement,
reading the *Necrofile*
before the next power meeting.

In Armani sunglasses,
it's hard to know what the women are thinking.
Probably about how hot the men look,
and how happy they are that
the Great Gender Reversal finally took place—
if only for a minute.

This is my beer commercial
& I don't have to apologize
for turning men into sex objects;
In this parallel universe
men enjoy being sex objects.

And a fabulous postmodern ending:
the women reveal themselves as Ad Execs,
who are drawing up a brilliant campaign
about men & women & beer
where the women are wearing Gucci,
& the men expose their perfect pecs.

CLASSIFIED:

You are a blue-eyed Aryan boy,
physically fit, no tattoos,
an Anglican man, a Baptist,
a WASPish German blonde.

At fourteen I flirted with a Satanic
guitarist from Louisville with long
oval nails and hair in his eyes singing
"Johnny Be Good" to an empty room.

I never wanted any part of Abraham,
but dreamed of eloping with Kurt,
hygienic and fatherly, someone I can burn
into with defiance, all my great rebellions.

An orphan 19 years and still
I need to madden my parents
who wore suffering and success
in 18 carat stars.

THEORIZING THE POSTMODERN

She slipped her hand in his, squeezed it

Postmodernism flau(n)ts the medium
ruptures contingent reality

He withdrew his, bored, lit a cigarette

We can't exist in ambiguity indefinitely.
Are we narrative junkies or do we crave
a little philosophy with our entertainment?

She stifled an urge to cry, bit her lip
until she tasted blood

Take a clever premise
& layer it, separate the idea
from its execution; execute the idea

She kissed him
pungent pomegranate
(she never withheld sexual flavours)

A painted diva bleeds like a religious icon—
he calls her a hoax—

Watch your own response
to a film; a novel; a "work of art"

photographs of body parts
in formaldehyde,
dolls wearing sexual prostheses

It's all subjective, narrative's a toy
weapon, a fish spilled from its bowl
gaping
A poem is already verse running free
words hung like wallpaper

And then she kissed him
she knew exactly what he wanted—
Passion!

That's what this poem is missing
Can you be detached &
simultaneously passionate?

> *And then she divined what*
> *he wanted, what it was he craved.*
> *She gutted the fish*
> *donned the prosthetic,*
> *ripped the head off the*
> *baby doll*
> *& spat in his face.*
> *He laughed, applauded & called her an artiste.*

SMOOTH AS PEARLS

The last one hated ponytails and socks
in bed, the porn in the machine, the fake
tits a rip-off. I wore pumps, silver

to bed, long red claws and a bustier.
The fake breasts, moaning fake, the nails
scratching his fake back, fake, but the sex

real, definitely real. I ought to be paid
for the costume dramas, the electrolysis,
psychoanalysis, smooth

as pearls, within, without. Next time, I'll wear
red socks to bed, a long ponytail. I'll be ancient
in animal skins with bones in my hair.

TAKE ME

He reaches out big, workman hands
lone-wolf arms tense & needy—
take me, he implores,
with my baggage,
insecurities, carpel tunnel syndrome.

Work your woman, earth mother, Goddess-
power magic, and make me whole.

Take my full head of tall dark—
to the cleft in a jaw that could cut cheese.

Mend my insides.
I'll give you what I withheld
all these years—
please, anoint me with your post-graduate
approval, and petite, sensuous mouth.

I reach out manicured hands:
take me, with all my
unmet expectations, overblown desires,
& make me scream. Overwhelm my
intellectualized craving to be loved.

Obliterate all these years of therapy:
drag me
by my hair & pull me into the cave.

EVEN DIVAS GET THE BLUES

Sapphire—
a quick flash of iris, before he turns to walk away

Aqua—
when she dissolved there, took a swim in him

Cobalt—
when eyes turned darker, darker still

Blue-black
mascara, pooling under her eyes
even divas get the blues

He pulled a trench coat close around his neck
chiaroscuro lighting framed their faces
half grey, half light
He ran long fingers through her hair,
said he loved her, but she didn't believe him.

It was all too *film noir*
too out-of-the-blue
She was walking a thin line between
falling in love and drowning
under the blue ice, so insubstantial—
no place to stand she could call terra firma

She wondered why she bothered at all!
Just because his hair smelled like Blue Mountain coffee
and every time they made love it was so blue
you could sell the tapes on the black market

She's talking a blue streak
how she's been stranded, careening down the luge of life
It's blue murder in her fantasies
She's going to kill that blue-collar boy

'Cause she sees blue, blue-on-blue
and when Divas get the blues—
it's the only colour worth mentioning

It was a question of fate, of a thing divined

on the Hollywood blue screen behind the lines
Fake backdrop, real passion
The tyranny of love took hold
purple-blue—
like love-making bruises or the crushed grapes of the
Cabernet
they drank that first time

You can't walk on blue he said—
sky or water
It was true enough
blue unfolded like liquid, like time

Bluegrass they heard in that little dive
in the middle of nowhere
where they danced a two-step
He raked her over with peacock eyes
called her a Diva
and it wasn't a compliment
Told her it was time to put her blue-suede Monolo's
on eBay & pay the hydro bill
'cause there was a chill in her studio apartment

He couldn't pay for the Armani's, the Pucci's, the Gucci's
even if they were Malaysian knockoffs
It was all too blue-blooded for him
after all, he was just a trumpet player
who liked to go to the track
no money left after that

I'm no Diva, just a woman with style
she said, though she knew
she was Diva through and through
Proud to be diva

Even Divas get the blues she told him
pouting, petulant, wooing him all over again

with those baby blues
But he wasn't listening
he'd picked up his horn
was 3 bars into a 12-bar sequence
the night was young.

She had a bottle of Bombay Sapphire Gin
sharp blue cheese and the midnight-blue neckline of her
velvet dress
plunged way down to *there*.

Oh yeah, even Divas get the blues—
one shade at a time.

OF COURSE THE POPCORN HELPS, TOO

Life doesn't translate easily into film.
It takes all kinds of subtle
and drastic manipulation
to turn tedium—
punctuated by tragedy and happy stop-frames—
into something watchable.

Section 3

OFF-LIMITS

ANIMAL PASSION

I dreamt a small black weasel
made love to me
and I enjoyed it, furtively.

I developed feelings for the weasel;
its claws and feet scratched me
but it had big, black, compassionate eyes
and a tenacious tongue.

The affair troubled me
so I put him in a crate
while I decided what to do.

When he escaped,
I felt that the only weasel
capable of loving me
had gotten away.

A FEW TERMINAL D'S

I am falling into bed
falling for you, on you,
your arms, questions, open ended.

My cat is dying. I am poised
between nightmares and a soaring
round of "Can't Get You Out of My Head."

Kylie Minogue is wearing
my nightgown. No life without contrast,
or some such platitude, no real

meaning to life without death—
and love can't be felt without
famine, an extended

period of aloneness. A friend tells me the terminal
D's are critical to poetry (like *loved* and *dead*).
I dreamed that my cat's life passed through

me and I moaned. Reaching out, you were
there, gently breathing, dreaming melancholy blonde
dreams right beside me, our bodies letters which

needed each other—consonants, vowels,
a few terminal D's, all blended together.

WILDLIFE

Photograph: yacht's prow, moored.
Man, woman, cat aboard
(a big bored cougar, dead centre).

Our smiles are as tight as the cat wrangler's rein.
Just before we joined the animal,
his handler asked us to give him a moment
to calm the cat down

My boyfriend resisted the urge to bolt
knowing full well this was a test of his masculinity.

It cost ten US dollars to pet the cougar
and receive this digital memento.
My boyfriend declined to touch the feline,
saying I was enough for him,
with my upturned eyes and overdeveloped incisors.

I'm not sure who was most exploited that day—
the cougar, my boyfriend, or me.

KLEZMER MUSIC ON CHRISTMAS EVE

Away from the reindeer and the tinsel
Jewish singles congregate
searching for that elusive Other.
and the faith is incidental to most of the secular Jews
who are looking for old-fashioned love
with all the trimmings.
Brimming with earnest hope
and cynical voices,
no I never come to this sort of event—never
This last, of course, said behind artfully painted red lips,
poised demurely, meeting a coffee cup, still smiling.

Group denial: we are here but
My friend dragged me along, didn't tell me what it was
Obvious hunger, but
we'll die before we admit it.

If life were a perpetual single's buffet,
I'd throw up from the indecency of desire.
Outside we keep on smiling.
I never want to pack myself in leather again, cleavage
provoking the shy.
I never want to expose myself to taut misery again,
hope contracted so tight
you can hear it snap when it breaks.

THIS WON'T HURT A BIT

When I'm in the dentist's chair
I think of sex.

Not sure why, but when my mouth is forced open
my mind wanders.

Or maybe it's because sex is the only thing
that distracts me to the point where the pain
melds into soft focus.

My new dentist, with a head of dark curls,
is young, gentle as a lamb. He charges a thousand
dollars an hour for a root canal. Yes, women,
that's the man to marry. Lawyers, doctors,
a poor second.

The chair goes up and back.
I close my eyes.

THE OLD ABANDONMENT

Why become my mother, giving
each man I date the third-degree,
        when there's no plastic on my furniture?

I put on a jeweled corset, danced and stripped
till 6 AM, in underground speakeasies,
        actors, dancers & fire-eaters.

Juggled photographer & chef,
drank, sniffed, played threesome, tempted
        the undead every Saturday night.

Another romantic comedy, my cat, huge
bowl of popcorn, purring, content. Nostalgic
        for curtain call smiles,

crying in dressing rooms, breaking
with a lover, hangovers, youth
        nothing but groping.

Now my apartment's off-limits, blood tests
before a shred of clothing hits the floor.

With the pleasure bleached out we're crisp, we're clean,
barren in the company of day-traders who,
        lonely and fearful, forget

the Epicurean rule. I long for the old abandonment,
for the sweat-soaked layers like snakeskin, the nights
        I'd lie down and give in.

MID-LIFE CRISIS IN FT. LAUDERDALE, REVISITED

Spring break has gone for the porn
look: girls in thong bikinis, navel
piercings and butt tattoos; the bikers and their Harleys
have taken over the strip by Lauderdale's beach.

I glimpsed a homeless man
from a block away, living down the lane
by the coastal condos, lacking sustenance or pity
in the balmy spring weather.

An itinerant mishmash of people live among
long-time residents who rarely see the blue
ocean or feel the lush tropical breezes—
dwelling in their climate-controlled condos,

stepping out of air-conditioned cars to air-
conditioned restaurants. Florida is wasted
on the old. This month they were clamouring
for living wills, death in the news

and on their minds. This place used to look like a set
for Spring Break Madness, kids falling drunk out of cars,
honking, hooting, flaunting
youth and insecurity all over the place. The residents

turned them out to Tampa or Daytona Beach. Now
you hear the occasional pulse of Black Eyed Peas,
see girls talk on cell phones, up to their waist in
the ocean. The biker owner of the Splish Splash bikini hut

tells me he'll give me 5 dollars off the price
of my suit if I'll table dance for him and his dogs, lying
bored, wearing bandanas and drooling
on the floor by the cash. He has an autographed photo

of Playboy's Miss August 2003 on display, smiling
thanks for your great store, Pete smile. I saw a man in a bikini
sunning alone on the beach, flat under his bikini top—
unmistakably male as the man dressed like a woman

at the 7-Eleven with Carmen Electra anatomy
and lashes. The jaw and Adam's apple gave him
away. They both made me sad
although saddest were the baby iguana and her mother,

transplanted to the lower level
of the underground parking,
slithering along
the concrete ramp. Context is everything.

When I'm here I imagine myself in a parallel life
where I take up residency in the ocean,
soft winds, the wild trees and foliage, saturated
flowers spinning out near the equator,

huge palms flapping, waving, telling me, *come here,*
stay here, where it's warm. I imagine myself in a sarong, my skin
espresso bean brown, tattoos of Mynah birds and iguanas
on my shoulders, back. I'd write by day, dance on the embezzler's

yacht by night. Maybe a job as waitress,
flinging conch soup at Hell's Angels and aging
lifeguards. Maybe pass a scuba-diving test and head down
to Key Largo. How can there be guns

in Margaritaville? Seems like a falling coconut
is the worst that could happen. And this visit, I swear
to God, Fernando from Costa Rica, gold chains around
his neck and wrist, sits down beside me, and in his gigolo

voice tells me I look *so beautiful*; he puts his hand
with diamond-encrusted pinky finger on my thigh.
The lifeguard's booth signals orange,
vida marina peligrosa, dangerous marine life. I brush him off

like sand flies, leave him smiling, his gold crowns glinting
in the sun. *25 cent drafts—Bikini Contest and Live Band at
        Beach Bums*
flies across the horizon when I meet Wilson, a chef and masseur,
who knows *everything* about satisfying a woman. Details may
        change
but nothing fundamental.

SECRET LIVES

The longing grows longer
at night, when we live in our right
brain. Other personalities emerge
while raccoons prowl. (Whole

families feed on the garbage
we leave rotting.) Chopin's
"Berceuse" incited me to want so much
more, to let in the sunlight and music,

enjoy shifts in classical mood, solitude.
(Nothing like a cat sitting on your
stomach to calm you.)
I'm looking to prove love right out

of existence, then resurrect it,
pull a rabbit out of your mouth.
Let's be civilized, let's be normal
about the whole thing. He's a saint

really and she's a homemaker, a goddess.
She wanted an artist, an opera singer
perhaps. But married a dentist.
We all give up something for that lump

in the bed. She gave up on romance,
he gave up on himself, and I relinquished
any part of it, to stand outside—
addicted to longing, this manufactured
world of light and dark, this fractured mirror.
I dip into it,
like holy water, imagine it could inform,
instruct   enlighten.

THE MEEK SHALL INHERIT

There's a mouse in my apartment
since my cat died. (Old, sick,
she still kept a nightly vigil.)
Now the mouse thinks it owns the place—
there are tell-tale holes in garbage bags
under my kitchen sink.

I've been told mice are nocturnal
so not to worry, but I'm nocturnal, too,
and we've faced each other once or twice.

The urge to jump on the nearest piece
of furniture is genetic. I borrowed my neighbour's pet
but the mouse went into hiding. It wasn't
going to fall for a rented cat.

Finally, my landlord hired a company
that placed little boxes of poisoned food
in strategic positions. A few days later,
I found a dead mouse carcass. It lay rigid
on the floor, accusing me.

My cat would have loved that mouse.
After hours of foreplay, she'd have killed it
with one swift vampire kiss
to the neck.

HOUSE OF CARDS

When one partner is dying
the sex between a couple
is unparalleled. The intensity

of each time —maybe the last—
takes the breath away.
The first time, too.

I lie down next to you
in a paper-thin sleep,
dreaming my eyelids open,
one bare foot on the floor.

THE PEAR

A still life gone awry,
the basin, the pear & me,
in tepid water, a naked fish.

I held a pear in a clenched fin,
splashed, screamed & the pear
sank. After what seemed
like hours, days, my tiny body

pruned in the water, my mother's voice
a kettle whistling, *But it's delicious,*
you must try a little bit. Sobs,
whimpers. Before our language—outrage,

a flailing of pudgy, aquatic limbs.
I remember a time before words
when my mother's face was
a bloated yellow pear.

MEDITATION ON A PHOTOGRAPH

We move one cubic centimetre to the left and the air feels a little different, colder perhaps. So we shift a little, back to where we were and the air is stagnant. We can't breathe.

My father's eyes were like a squirrel's, all shifty and uncomfortable. He couldn't hold your gaze for long. My mother's were blue-grey; they could be soft and they could harden in a second. Their eyes look out at me in photos now and I see different things. They don't look old any more. They look kind and happy.

There's a formal family photo on the wall above my desk. I'm about a year old, sitting on my mother's lap like a ventriloquist's dummy, or a big toy doll where you pull the string and her pudgy arms wave. My sister, about six, is a little ballerina in puffy pink sleeves, and my nine-year-old brother is wearing a suit with a little bowtie. My dad looks handsome, with a far-off gaze. The only person smiling is my mother. I wish I knew how to stop erosion and make what I have safe.

NONE OF THIS

My first Feb. 14th memory: our grade four Hebrew teacher
who raged, *SAINT Valentine's Day? We do not believe
in saints or saviors! Blasphemy! Hand them over!*

He seized hand-scrawled hearts
exchanged from girl to boy, boy to girl, ripped them
to a thousand profane pieces.

*Jews do not celebrate the glorification of saints. Do you think
this is funny? I will have none of this!*

Our ten-year-old hearts knew better.
He had the Torah, the Kabala, but we had recess
coming up. He couldn't stop us from loving.

WARNING SIGNS

With each the absence of love is different,
with each the absence of love is the same.

–Samuel Beckett

1.

I walk in my sleep
to reach you.
A huge, illegal pack of pit bulls
bark the way to you.
I put my head on the pillow and wait.

2.

A bible and a scale
under the bed. She knows where
to put her prayers.
Which came first,
the scale or the bible?
Thou shalt not eat cake—
the single girl's first commandment.

3.

I dreamed of your gentle nature
turned violent. You bounced her like a basketball
until she broke.
I left my wife, you said.

4.

All the biological
clocks in my apartment are set
to a different time.
But I am always late, regardless.

Section 4

AN AERIAL VIEW

THREE BODIES

Dedicated to Cobalt, 1988–2003

I.

There is an aerial view
I wish had been photographed:
Above my queen-sized bed, your
arms and mine entangled,

your body and mine breathing side
by side, and in that small crevice
between toes and ankles
is a small, frail bundle of fur,

safe, protected, just a week
before her death. She purrs lightly,
cuddling closer to the muted

breathing and warmth.
It is the last time there will ever
be three bodies in that bed—
grown cavernous overnight.

II.

Tiny grey ghosts slip
around each corner, whisper
on my sheets. The wind whips.
This apartment was a home when

you sidled up next to me,
nestled on a pillow. Nothing
but ashes. I am lost,
stacking up cans of food,

packing up your things for
the animal shelter. And that
other body is gone, a visitor
who left too

soon. The silence so loud
it cracks, I turn up the TV
and the heat.

AN EMAIL ABOUT THE OCEAN

He was holidaying at a beachside coastal town,
Tamil Nadu, India, south of Chennai (Madras).
Sitting in meditation, the surf's hypnotic
backdrop ruptured by the surge of water,
confused cries and shouts of villagers, tourists and fishers.

The ocean was everywhere, racing in and
overtaking his vision, his consciousness. Abating
for a moment, he caught his footing on a small ledge
and clung to it. Everything was lost:
passport, rupees, credit card, books, camera, clothes,
writing, eyeglasses, shoes.

Sometimes all we need is evidence, the words
of a friend who experiences.

He signs Aham Brahman Asmi.
Tsunami changed his name, millions
of others I never knew. Empathy sometimes needs a conductor.

PROVIDENCE, RHODE ISLAND

For Gabe

I went to Providence, streets called
Hope, Mary, Angel & Stephen.

A college town that bustles with self
importance, Brown's heritage buildings
display, proudly, small signs at
their entranceway: 1786, 1834.

Painted wood-frame construction,
New England pastels, pale yellow,
green, grey, Robin's egg blue.
Episcopal churches, their spires needling

through magnolia and crabapple
blossoms. Privileged young feet stride across
sidewalks of interlocking red brick, up and
down the hilly zigzags, backpacks in tow.

An army of freshman & sophomore ants
carrying boxes, empty out cluttered
dorm rooms, the acrid smell of spilled beer
soaked into carpets. They fill their parents' German cars,
heading home to the suburbs for the summer,
after the excitement, the intellectual rigour,
the drinking.

We hear how some students, on work-study programs
return disillusioned, at least one suicide attempt per term.
They cannot reconcile third-world misery with the beauty
of this idyll, this sleepy, silver-spooned hollow.

SONNET FOR JOHN

Empty space turned garden's resplendent trove.
Every facet of gleaming pleasure
increases, rich in word and deed to prove
that this map—your map—indicates treasure.

My heart, so long mute, surely gladdens
at the pure sight of you, proud and willful.
And your absence, counted in minutes can sadden—
still relishing moments sinful.

Countenance blushes, but the bees who sweeten
and make sticky love to each and every flower
won't give up, work tirelessly, brow-beaten
by the Queen, who like me, waits in her bower.

The sacred turn of love fades fast to sorrow;
Joy, dear, when I wake to you on the morrow.

THE ANGEL EFFECT

Aren't you dead? I ask. *No, honey. Your dad and I divorced. Didn't want you to know that, to lose your faith in love. So I went to live in Florida.* But it's later that you pick it apart. Sooner or later one parent or the other will be cruel, stupid or maddening, just as you remember. You want to shake them, pull your hair. He was probably buying 5 cases of sardines on special to save a dollar, or rolling his eyes and saying *of course I love you—don't be so dramatic* to my ten-year-old self. They leave you and you become an adult, *individuated*, who doesn't seem to need parental love. You grieve in your sleep and don't even remember your dreams. I scrawl 'dreamed about dad, again,' and figured I'd remember the rest.

TRANSCENDENCE

She wore her corsage everywhere.
The petals began to fall
but she didn't notice as she sat in the dark
watching people fall in & out of love—
she ate flowers with her popcorn, crying.

She watched a couple of pigeons from her
office at work. One clucked and paced
the narrow ledge, while the other
went out, gathering branches.

When she moved into her new apartment, the
first thing she bought was a pair of lovebirds.
She had to know that it was possible, had to see
it with her own eyes.

Every week she bought a fresh bunch of
tulips or daisies. The petals fell into
her cereal sometimes, and she tasted
hope in every mouthful.

`

PREVIOUSLY PUBLISHED POEMS:

Versions of these poems appeared in my first three chapbooks, *Vulnerable Positions, The Old Abandonment* and *Warning Signs*. Others appeared—and I thank their editors gratefully—in *Taddle Creek Magazine, Chiaroscuro, The Annex Echo, Existere, Kiss Machine, The Blue Ruin, Surface & Symbol, Ottawa/Toronto Word Exchange, Eye Weekly* and *Word*.

NOTES:

"A Few Terminal D's" won second place in the *Word: Canada's Magazine for Readers and Writers* 2004 Literary Contest.

"This is My Beer Commercial" placed second in *Eye Weekly*'s "Pitchers of Poetry" Contest, 1998.

"An Incident" was written during Stuart Ross' Poetry Boot Camp, 2004.

"Even Divas Get the Blues" was commissioned by Fern Lindzon for her Jazz concert of the same name at the Heliconian Club, Nov. 25, 2003.

"An E-mail about the Ocean" was inspired by J. Dennie's surreal personal account of surviving the 2004 Tsunami.

ACKNOWLEDGEMENTS:

I'm hugely grateful to the Toronto Arts Council and Ontario Arts Council for their generous financial assistance.

ONTARIO ARTS COUNCIL
CONSEIL DES ARTS DE L'ONTARIO

I am bursting to thank Halli Villegas, my biggest supporter and the best publisher a writer could ask for. Ray Hsu, as editor, deserves more than I can repay, for his penetrating intelligence at all times. To David Bigham, whose photographic and design work scintillates. And to Carleton Wilson, for going that extra creative mile.

So many colleagues and friends contributed to making this book more than a figment of my imagination: Clara Blackwood, Carolyn Clink, David Clink, Sandra Kasturi, Souvankham Thammavongsa, and the other fine poets of the Algonquin Square Table. Al Moritz, our group moderator and mentor, who gives so much and asks so little, you are greatly appreciated.

To my wonderful friends and family, who urge me forward every day, and give me a leg up, especially Gary Bourgeois, Colleen Flood, Catherine Graham, Fern Lindzon, Ginny McFarlane, Dick Wallin, Sheilah Wallin, and Heather Wood.

ABOUT THE AUTHOR:

Myna Wallin is a poet, prose writer, small press publisher and radio host. She has been co-publisher of BELIEVE YOUR OWN PRESS with David Clink, publishing poetry chapbooks since 2001. Myna hosts *In Other Words* on CKLN 88.1 FM, interviewing writers from across Canada. She holds a Master of Arts degree in English Literature from the University of Toronto and works as a freelance editor. This is her first book of poetry.

MEMBER OF SCABRINI GROUP

Québec, Canada
2006